Lend Me Your Ear	7
Deliberative Bodies	16
Conflict	20
Power	30
Cognitive Dissonance	38
Coalitions	48
Public Hearing	56
Meeting The Challenge	63
Getting Your Proposal Heard	67
Preamble	72
Facilitative Leadership	74
Communication	81
Road Blocks	85
Listen	91
Assertion	97
Problem Solving	103
Time To Govern	111

DEDICATION

TO LYNNE, ALEX & ANDREW
FOR LENDING ME THEIR TIME
AS WELL AS THEIR EARS

AUTHOR'S NOTE:
ALL SIMILARLY FRAMED QUOTATIONS
CONTAINED IN THIS BOOK ARE FROM
JAMES MADISON'S FEDERALIST NO.10.

ENDORSEMENTS

"*Lend Me Your Ear* is an indispensable tool for anyone doing business in the public arena."
—Joshua Davis, Esquire

"*Lend Me Your Ear* dissects the nature of the political beast and unravels the quagmire of how to make real progress with public boards and administrative bodies."
—Jack Englert, Criterion Development Partners

"*Lend Me Your Ear* is the guidebook we all need to succeed in the public arena. This pithy, witty book should be your compass."
—Chris Gabrieli

"Michael has described citizen participation and all of its nuances. Based on his years of experience on both sides of the aisle, he knows how to reach consensus."
—Pamela G. McDermott, President McDermott Ventures

"*Lend Me Your Ear* identifies the characteristics and obstacles that exist in the public arena and offers insight towards improving discourse."
—Diane McMonagle-Glass, Assistant General Counsel, Real Estate CVS Caremark Corporation

"As Council President, Michael J. O'Halloran's leadership and manner fostered an atmosphere in this chamber that enabled us to generate more light than heat."
—Robert Waddick J.D., Waltham City Councillor

"In the public arena, interpersonal dynamics govern the outcomes that are generated through the communicative process. Effective interpersonal skills foster the rapport that is necessary to advance ideas and proposals, in short, for being heard."

MICHAEL J. O'HALLORAN

LEND ME YOUR EAR
A Guide for Getting Heard and Understood in the Public Arena

An old adage states that we have two ears and one tongue, therefore we should listen *twice* as much as we speak. The message conveys more than the numerical advantage of ears—listening more than speaking furthers the communication process of exchanging thoughts and messages. In addition, transmission whether verbal, via emails or texting, is more than a one-way transaction. For information to be received as intended, it requires that a connection be established. In William Shakespeare's immortal play *Julius Caesar,* the character Mark Antony says the often quoted lines: "Friends, Romans, countrymen, lend me your ears…" Antony, orating at Caesar's funeral, made a connection with his audience. Antony, himself a great leader, says to his disciples: "I am like you, I know your dreams and desires, so please listen." He spoke to the Romans rather than *at* them.

"But that's great for Shakespeare," you might say, "but this is reality." True, but effective communication, and relating to your subject, is essential for success in our daily lives. Today, however, we often use the singular figure of speech, asking people to "lend me your ear" to not only connect with the listener but to request attention.

In the public arena, interpersonal dynamics govern the outcomes that are generated through the communicative process. Effective interpersonal skills foster the rapport that is necessary to advance ideas and proposals, in short, for being heard. Whether you find yourself before Congress, a public board at city hall, or before the board of your condominium or neighborhood association, you must deal with the unique challenges that those who appear before deliberative bodies encounter. Deliberative bodies are made up of people who are either elected or appointed to a public position for the purposes of making decisions on behalf of a larger group of people, such as a community association, town, or state population. They are charged with rendering careful consideration of the matters that are before them. This process, however, can be confounded by the complexities of the communication process and human nature.

Knowing this places special appreciation for the above adage and the potential to evoke shared interdependence. And so, without further ado, lend me your ear…

EACH year, billions of dollars are spent trying to educate deliberative bodies on proposals that meet the public need. Proposals related to housing, retail, food services, the environment, and education: all significant community proposals. And yet, very little education is achieved, and even less information is exchanged.

More often than not, the public process produces more friction than fusion, and more fiction and faction, than it does truth and action. Our nation's community-based, decision-making boards are mired down by gamesmanship; agendas and partisanship have rendered our deliberative bodies listening impaired. Hearing is occurring, but is listening? Our public hearing process, in and of itself, produces little listening and more opportunity for talking, or should I say, shouting, in order to build coalitions, to grandstand, and to distract from the very hearing process that is intended to promote listening.

The problems with our hearing process are, in part, the result of a human tendency to create conflict. The framers of our nation's Constitution recognized that human nature would be active in our government, and they took into account the inherent human propensity for conflict and its consequences.

James Madison wrote in the Federalist Papers:

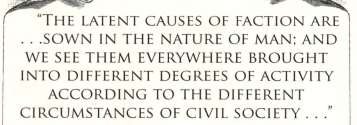

"THE LATENT CAUSES OF FACTION ARE . . . SOWN IN THE NATURE OF MAN; AND WE SEE THEM EVERYWHERE BROUGHT INTO DIFFERENT DEGREES OF ACTIVITY ACCORDING TO THE DIFFERENT CIRCUMSTANCES OF CIVIL SOCIETY . . ."

Anyone who has ever appeared before a public body, as a petitioner, developer, community member, or official has witnessed firsthand how alliances, or factions as I frequently refer to them, interfere with thoughtful decision-making. These factions interfere with a petitioner's ability to engage public officials in the dialog that is necessary for the advancement of ideas and implementation of proposals. This results in decisions and outcomes that reflect more emotion than substance; dialog deprivation renders outcomes that do not appear to be based on proposed subject matter. The fractionalization of our public bodies, whether a city council, a board of alderman or selectman, a planning/zoning board, community association, or a condo or school board is on the rise, becoming more common and extending beyond any historical partisan political faction. Today's factions are fluid and their composition changes are based upon the circumstances of the moment. Whether formed at the coffee shop, ball field, church, bar, garden club, or chat room, a faction's origin is the same: people coming together to interact, reducing the seclusion that the information age of text messaging, emailing, and faxing has created. Seeking inclusion, these alliances are formed and brought into the public boardrooms of our society, and then are further ratified through the deliberative process of our legislative boards that provide an arena for public gathering and discourse.

While many of these factions are unobservable to the momentary guest petitioner, they may be aware of an undercurrent that is influencing their proposal. Those who appear before our public boards seeking to inform and participate in the deliberative process—in order to meet some perceived public need—are affected by the subtle formation of factions, conflict, and communication. Petitioners need a current meter to understand what is really going on beneath the surface, and to develop the process skills that can allow parties to manage and improve the ebb and flow of discourse.

Conflict is often forged onto the public stage when officials seeking to connect with colleagues or constituents ask a petitioner a question that is intended to appease other board or community members. The question itself conveys to other board members, or even to the public, that "I'm like you," or as Barney the purple dinosaur would sing, "I love you, you love me, we're a happy family." Often in the political arena, only those who share its melody understand the tune that is sung or played out, through words or actions. For the petitioner, the question furnishes an opportunity to inform and persuade their audience that the proposal being presented is for the good of the community. By giving a thoughtful answer, the petitioner assumes that they can overcome any negative thoughts, enlighten the questioner, and be on their way to approval, however fleeting. As Madison asserted in his *Federalist Papers,* however, the public good is secondary to individual interests:

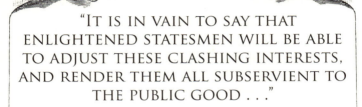

> "IT IS IN VAIN TO SAY THAT ENLIGHTENED STATESMEN WILL BE ABLE TO ADJUST THESE CLASHING INTERESTS, AND RENDER THEM ALL SUBSERVIENT TO THE PUBLIC GOOD . . ."

Madison sought to balance clashing interests through the system of checks and balances so that no one individual interest can be asserted at the expense of the communal benefit. Our system seeks to balance the clashing of interests within and between our government structures. But what about the impact of social and political interest on individuals who stand before the body politic? The atmospherics of our deliberative bodies often produce dynamics unrelated to the matters that are brought before them. Standing there in the public sea, petitioners cannot remove the wind but they can change its direction by providing leadership that facilitates thoughtful decision-making. As a petitioner, you cannot change the formal structure of our public boards, but you can alter its impact.

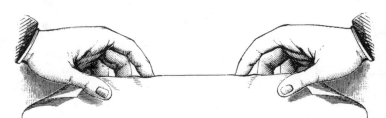

"THE INFERENCE TO WHICH WE ARE BROUGHT IS THAT THE CAUSES OF FACTION CANNOT BE REMOVED AND THAT RELIEF IS ONLY TO BE SOUGHT IN THE MEANS OF CONTROLLING ITS EFFECTS."

This book seeks to provide the reader with the means to understand and control the effects that the modern public arena produces, and for you to govern your behavior when standing before the body politic. Those who place themselves before our nation's deliberative boards must have a personal constitution and skills necessary for being heard, and more importantly, to be understood in a political context.

"DELIBERATIVE BODIES are charged with rendering careful consideration of the matters that are before them. This process, however, can be confounded by the complexities of the communication process and human nature."

MICHAEL J. O'HALLORAN

JAMES MADISON'S thoughts about the inclinations of human nature, and in particular "statesmen," were prescient. His keen awareness and foresight of *how* people behave and conduct themselves was not only observant, but also prescriptive. Madison understood that people, enlightened or not, would face conflicts when seeking to balance the varied needs and interest of the public. Recognizing the challenge public servants would have with adjusting to the "clashing of interest," Madison prescribed an elixir in our constitution by spelling out the separation of powers in order to remedy any one official or body from taking actions, which may be based on inflamed public opinion or subjectivity, from coming to fruition without consultation and deliberation of other branches of government.

As a petitioner before a public board, you must build on Madison's insight into human nature and appreciate the unique "personality" of the political arena and its actors. The modern statesman—whether they be a selectman, city councilor, legislator, school board, zoning or planning board member—are subjected to the same external influences that Madison wrote about. However, today's clashing of interests produces a percussion, which at times can be deafening. Today, officials find themselves intertwined with the public in a manner very different from what was experienced by earlier public servants. The space that the prairie provided, written letters that were delivered on horseback, and the slower pace of everyday life enabled greater consideration of issues and one's subsequent feelings. Today, inflamed thought is fueled by the lightning speed of technology and the public's proximity to officials. Unlike the pony express mail system of yesteryear, few barriers slow the delivery of an email or blog which usually incites a knee-jerk reaction instead of an insightful one. The challenges that surround the body politic—and the officials who occupy public positions—are not only external from the public, but also internal from within the political body and one's self. The voices in one's head can be as conflicting as those coming from their peers.

The atmosphere of our political arena contains many disparate particles: Conflict, Power, Cognitive Dissonance, and Coalitions orbit the arena and the public hearing process. For your proposal to be heard—and more importantly listened to—you must begin with the end in mind: facilitating leadership, enabling communication, and using problem-solving techniques.

An awareness of the times, challenges faced by public officials, and characteristics of decision-making boards are essential for anyone appearing before a public body. As a petitioner, you must use this awareness to guide your actions and increase deliberation in order to advance your proposal and reduce costs.

CONFLICT

"To understand the body politic, one must delve beneath the superficial in order to appreciate the underlying sources of power and conflict surrounding the deliberative arena."

Michael J. O'Halloran

CONFLICT is a universal phenomenon: it is everywhere. However, what is one person's struggle with events or ideas is another's harmony. Idiosyncratic factors exist in individuals and often play themselves out on the public stage, requiring you as a petitioner to offer a dedicated response in order to address both individual and group concerns. At its base, conflicts are most often seen as being fundamentally similar. Factors such as culture, power, resources, gender, security, and identity are all sources of conflict. However, conflicts that occur in the public arena have an emphasis on identity and power and have many stages. Conflict is too often met with avoidance, aggression, or dismissal.

In the public arena, conflict is traced back to the messenger—who is either validated or shot. The "killing of the messenger" originated with the writings of Sophocles in Ancient Greece and has now been adapted to today's technology. But for the killing blow, the blog has replaced the sword. Whether coming from community groups or city hall, petitioners are inevitably impacted by conflict and must guard against a "one size fits all" approach to resolving it. One method should not be applied universally. What resonated in *one* community is not necessarily applicable in another. A developer may conduct a neighborhood meeting in one community, which serves to clarify misperceptions about their proposal, and as a result of the meeting, receives community support. In another town, a similar meeting may provide an opportunity for political grandstanding because the meeting serves as an unintentional forum for a rising political aspirant who intends on running for office during the next election, and therefore uses your meeting as an opportunity to raise other issues or incite the crowd.

Conflicts that occur in the public arena are parochial and patriarchal; they can be narrowly restricted to local concerns and are often rooted in the perceived problems of the past. Lore and political lineage add complexity and confusion for the outsider trying to understand how their particular matter is connected both in historical and practical terms. Public arena disputes are further impacted by public observation. In this arena, the level and impact of conflict is increased because much of the conflict that is displayed is carried out in front of an audience, television camera, or news reporter. In the public arena, political- and community-based conflict is rooted in identity. Matters of face, both saving and losing, are always present and often overshadow substantive discussion. How conflicts are handled greatly affects how matters are perceived, and ultimately received, by community decision makers. These decision makers operate in unique and conflicted settings. Public discourse is structured and governed by the rules of the body convening the meeting. Organizational tools, such as the often-used handbook *Robert's Rules of Order* for running meetings effectively and efficiently further restrain expression and impact intention. This is in contrast to the unwieldy, natural airing of concerns and expression of emotion that takes place in the unfettered conversations of our everyday lives. Conflict in the public arena is a result of the people involved, the setting, the structure, the politics, and the matters of power and identity. The public arena has variables that are different from everyday conflicts.

Such as…

☛ Numbers of Parties:

Many different groups and constituencies exist in a public setting. The groupings add to the complexity, but also create opportunities for building relationships and solving community needs.

☞ Atmospherics:

Some atmospheric factors include: the location for public discussion (whose turf is the meeting on?): the history of the space (has this been a location that people felt comfortable in? Have they been heard in this space?), and seating arrangements. (Is it circular or linear seating with rows of the public facing a conference table made up of board members in one space and petitioners in another, creating an Us versus Them dynamic?) Some other atmospherics to consider are sound and acoustics of the area, as well as room temperature.

☞ Context:

What else is going on in the public arena while your issue's matter is being considered? Things to consider: if it is election time, if a town meeting is coming up, or if there are controversial proposals or fighting amongst board members.

☞ Number of Issues:

A greater number of issues are present in the public arena, economic matters such as taxation, budgetary, public safety, education, public health, and so on. The multitude of issues that are before deliberative bodies can make it more difficult for your proposal to be considered separate from everything else that is going on, but also provide more opportunities to reach agreements when the meeting of community concerns can be bundled with other issues.

☞ Power:

Power exists both formally and informally throughout the public arena and is often not balanced. It is often achieved by gaining a position, spearheading a cause, influencing events, and outcomes. In the political arena, how officials act or react to proposals before them determines the power they may achieve or squander.

☞ Effective Third-Party Intervention:

Opportunities for impartial intervention by a third-party are limited by the control exerted by public bodies and their power to render decisions.

☞ Audiences:

In the public arena, you are not alone. The media and members of the public are often sitting "front and center" as you are trying to explain your proposal. This provides a level of transparency, but also increases posturing as actors on the public stage perform for the crowd.

☞ Reputation:

What is the reputation of the board that you are appearing before? Is it known for collaboration or confrontation? What is your reputation? If you're a national entity, how have your dealings with other communities shaped your reputation?

☞ Trust:

The public is rightfully concerned with the reliability of commitments that are made by those in the public arena. Officials, petitioners, consultants, and so on are all challenged as to the veracity of their statements and enforceability of commitments made. These concerns create many obstacles to the open dialog that is needed to advance a proposal. Petitioners and officials must work together to forge a lasting trust.

☞ Institutions and Bureaucracies:

The bureaucratic structures offer a web of inertia that stymies progress. Often in the public arena, many individuals have to "sign off" on your proposal. This can lead to officials stating, "I cannot sign off on this until you first get clearance from department B and C." When you go to B and C, they say official A must first sign off on the proposal. Then round and round you go as officials search for support within the "institution" for your proposal.

It may not been your intention to ride the ferris wheel at the public fair, but you can use the height and slow motion of this apparatus to help you gain perspective and influence. First, we must continue to understand the underlying mechanics that drive the public arena. Then we will progress in this book to establish a personal constitution as a vehicle to govern your actions in the public arena.

The gears that rotate in the public arena often grind to a halt when petitioners find their proposals impacted by other issues before the board, the characteristics of the membership, and precedent. What other issues are on the agenda with your matter? Is there any relationship between your proposal and other agenda items? For example, you represent a National Drug Store chain that seeks approval to allow their store to stay open past midnight. However, Any Town, USA, for example, has a local restriction that prohibits any business from staying open past midnight. On the same evening that your employer National Drugs is on the agenda, you find that Gas Station Nation is also on the very same agenda to allow its station to stay open past midnight. Your first thought might be that there is strength in numbers: if there are other businesses with a need to stay open past midnight, the town must recognize this need and grant us both approvals. However, in our fictitious Any Town, there is a large, elderly population who use prescription drugs, and who would not only like to have them available for purchase after midnight, but would also like the comfort of knowing that in the wee hours of the morning they could call their helpful and kind pharmacist if they had any concerns or questions. You represent National Drugs and initially feel comforted not having to go it alone in seeking relief from the time restrictions. However, you discover that the Gas Station is located next to one of the largest elderly housing complexes in the area and is currently a point of contention because of the noise that is generated from the gas station during "normal" business hours. Kids pull in with their radios blaring, doors are slamming, people are talking, and cars are roaring out of the parking lot. It is speculated that these problems will only get worse after midnight when all the "hooligans" are out. So what appeared to be an advantage of not going it alone is now an obstacle, inadvertently entwined in a very emotional public discussion. National Drugs is now connected to Gas Station Nation under "Future Agenda Items – 24 hr. Operations."

Other issues on an agenda can give your item an unexpected audience. A budgetary matter involving cuts in public safety may bring out a crowd and security concerns about having fewer police on the street. This crowd will take notice of other agenda items, particularly ones that may in some way help their argument. A business open during the night, especially one that sells drugs and attracts loiterers, could easily translate into a need for police surveillance. Other agenda items or issues in the public arena often have an unintended impact on your particular issues. The issues in contention, while different, have the characteristics of an adversary when they can be linked together. The context of your proposal will no longer be judged individually, but on its relationship to other issues.

POWER

"You must learn to appreciate both the unique dynamic that exists within deliberative bodies and the intrinsic tension that is ever-present. Members of deliberative bodies must constantly balance the relations between one another, the public, and other strongly opposing elements."

MICHAEL J. O'HALLORAN

MAGNETS, as defined by *The American Heritage Dictionary*, are bodies "that attract iron and other materials by virtue of a surrounding field of force produced by the motion of its atomic electrons and the alignments of its atoms." The amazing power that causes magnets to attract matter is the same force that, when faced with comparable power, repels with aggression. You can hold in each hand this magical power, but when you try to put them together, the forces fight one another. Briefly, you can maintain equilibrium, but soon your hands shake, producing a reflexive tremor that ultimately forces one magnet to ascend while the other descends. This phenomenon exists not only in natural science, but in political science as well. The body politic produces a similar source of conflict and tension, and its impact is felt both internally, amongst officials, and externally by those who appear before Our Nation's deliberative bodies.

As a petitioner before a public body, you must recognize that the decision makers that you stand before are part of a larger political continuum, and their actions are often influenced by the unique history of the decision-making body and its resulting culture. For example, you may find yourself before a public board trying to make a case for the need of a "youth or cultural center" in your community. As a petitioner, you approach the podium in the public arena, appearing before a public board with the power to grant such a request. You make your case passionately, and hopefully in a persuasive manner, only to be told at the conclusion of your remarks, "Thank you" as in *"Next!"*

You are stunned. You anticipated discourse, an actual conversation between you, the proponent of an idea that will benefit the community, and the elected or appointed officials who responsibility it is to carry out the will of the people. It may be the intention of the public officials to do just that: facilitate the wishes of the public. However, our public boards are not only composed of the people that you are standing before but are also composed, in spirit and deed, by those who in previous generations who sat in the very seats as the decision makers that you now stand before. The experience of the past has taught this body a lesson. That is, after a petitioner makes their case, the decision makers suggest that the matter will be placed "on a future agenda and that your issue can only be heard at this time" and not discussed or acted upon. Why is that? When we dig deeper in this example, we find that previous board members of the decision-making body found that if they responded immediately to a petitioner's request, by action or dialog, they would lose power and be at a disadvantage. They may not have all the facts or may give in to the pressure of a large crowd of citizens. The board members may feel rightfully unprepared to respond to your request. After all, you as the petitioner had not only prepared the script but also, more often than not, assembled an audience to support your petition. You have not only information power, but also resource and people power on your side. For the public body charged with the responsibility to act, if they chose, on your proposal, power resides in their "position" and ability to control the process.

The presence of power is felt by anyone who finds themselves in the political arena—it is conveyed by the architecture, trappings, historical statutes, and renderings. Its force is enhanced by the structured nature of communication that is imposed on you, the petitioner, using forms, deadlines, submittal requirements, and the time limits that are imposed on speech when appearing before a deliberative body. This power is legitimate and has been granted to selected individuals through either appointment or direct elections to the positions that they hold. Power exists both formally and informally throughout the body politic and its impact is experienced by you, the petitioner, on an intermittent basis depending on whom may occupy positions of power and how a individual political actor may exercise power over you, your proposal, or those you represent.

Governmental bodies may contain all the formal vestiges of power, but the execution is idiosyncratic to the individuals who occupy governmental positions.

Power that is derived from the unique characteristics that an individual office holder may possess is often greater than the formal power that is bestowed upon them by the position they hold. The very nature of an individual's personality and charisma can be awesome, and is enhanced by the position they hold. Those who occupy elected positions in the public arena are, as our founders intended, come from all walks of life: entrepreneurs, doctors, chefs, lawyers, accountants, day care providers, engineers, and so on. Often, proposals that are before these office holders are about subject matters that some of these individuals may be "experts" in. A proposal to construct a building to house a biomedical tenant may be before a body that happens to have a biochemist on the board as well as an architect. Such officials who are deliberating on your proposal would be viewed among their colleagues and the community as being uniquely qualified to deliberate on your proposal; being viewed are the resident "experts" on such a matter instantly increases their power.

The public arena also produces opportunities for its members to possess and gain other types of power. Resource, prestige, and transactional power are ever-present. Consider, for example, the following officials who are a resource to their colleagues, albeit campaign assistance, help one another on particular subject matters or provide constituencies to support a colleague's legislative goals. This support, offered by a fellow official, could be an invaluable resource that adds to the power base of the person giving and receiving the support. Prestige power also finds a home in the political arena. Politicians often rely on the prestige that a fellow politician may bring to them. Inviting a prestigious colleague to a political fundraiser to speak on their behalf can add luster and dollars to their campaign war chest. If a political actor is a war hero, sports legend, or local celebrity, their life experience adds power to an already powerful position. The public arena also trades in the currency of transactions, helping one another gain positions and advance legislation; all of the above mentioned are sources of power. You must understand these sources and its impact on your proposal.

Many public boards engage in "power-based" leadership styles that seek to assert, gain, and acquire power. This forceful leadership style adds to the fractionalization of board members who often meet force with equal force and, like magnets, after a period of positioning, one ascends while the other descends or declines.

No matter which fraction may win or lose an argument, legislative achievement or parliamentary fight, the battle itself tends to produce an outcome that results in casualties that inadvertently inflict latent backlash among officials internally, and are often carried over externally when petitioners, like you, appear before a fractured body.

COGNITIVE DISSONANCE

"Public officials often take positions that are in conflict with their own beliefs in order to meet the demands of either colleagues or the public. This vague sense of public/private persona leads to conflicting views as public officials are forced to wear multiple masks in order to play the resulting ideological roles that society as his producer casts them in."

Michael J. O'Halloran

THE interplay resulting in conflicting needs and desires exists not only externally when dealing with other people or establishments, but also internally, when an individual takes action on behalf of constituencies that are in conflict with their own individual or professional beliefs. The result of this is *cognitive dissonance:* the condition or conflict that results in anxiety and frustration when one individual acts in a manner that is inconsistent with his or her beliefs. One example of such dissonance may be working for a company that creates pollution, despite being a strong advocate for clean air.

Public officials often take positions that are in conflict with their own beliefs in order to meet the demands of either colleagues or the public. The cumulative effect of taking such positions leads many officials to feel as if they are merely "taking orders," often at an alarming rate, similar to the kid with the headset at the neighborhood fast-food, drive-thru window. The passionate voices that once shaped our constitution have been slowly replaced by figurative "call boxes" like the generic, fast-food question, "May I take your order please?" Our society has created a dynamic where officials often substitute original thought for order taking, resulting in acidity between themselves, the voters, and their own ideals. The popular, fast food commercial jingle of "special orders don't upset us" now contaminates the body politic—where the media, voters, and special interests sing a similar tune to their chosen representatives: "giving orders doesn't upset us." The public saying, "Serve us," has replaced public service. Like most things that the public seeks to consume, their appetite and the resulting "orders" that are placed with our public officials are often indigestible by the body politic, and that is perhaps the reason why so few people today run for office, or why there is such voter apathy displayed by the dismal turnouts on Election Day.

This "order-placing" and "order-taking" phenomenon has increased the public's cynicism toward those who hold public office—because the relationship between the two is often mistaken as a recipe for leadership. Leadership is, after all, is commensurate with "influence," but the influence that the public has on elected officials should not come from the public "giving orders." Leaders exert influence and the citizenry should inform their actions. Those who appear before the body politic must recognize the pressures that exist on public officials when carrying out their public duties in what is often a cynical atmosphere. The cynicism that exists towards public officials has taken on its own life. Today's cynics have replaced the once healthy perspective of balancing an open mind with a dose of skeptical contemplation with a belief that those who serve as elected or appointed officials is primarily motivated by self interests. Sadly, too often this viewpoint has overtaken how a public official are perceived.

Public officials whose public services were once seen as "for the people, by the people" and whom came to being as servants "of the people," are now viewed as employees and political laborers, and as such, are expected to perform services that are dictated by their employer—the electorate—who makes the official's employment possible. Increasingly, it is expected by the electorate that the political officials' actions are to be guided externally by society and internally through self as public survival necessitates. The implied message is that if the official wants to get re-elected or reappointed then the official will do as the electorate tells him or her. This is not how our forefathers had envisioned public service, nor how other significant thinkers of our time sought to reflect the public will. Engraved on the building of the John Joseph Moakley Court House in Boston is this inscription by Justice Felix Frankfurter:

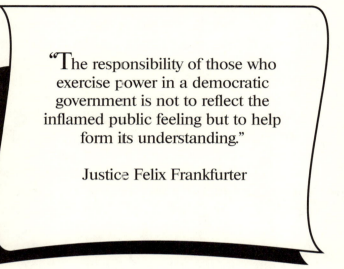

"The responsibility of those who exercise power in a democratic government is not to reflect the inflamed public feeling but to help form its understanding."

Justice Felix Frankfurter

As a result of the public nature of the political official's job, and the modern day demands that are placed on the officials, there exists a haze between where their personal life and views begins and society's collective projected identity ends. Public officials are consistently challenged to carry out what is expected of them by the electorate, under the guise that this is what it means to be a leader. The pressure that the electorate employer applies seeks to render the individual thoughts and actions of political officials secondary to the whims of the public. This vague sense of public/private persona leads to conflicting views as public officials are forced to wear multiple masks in order to play the resulting ideological roles that society as his producer casts them in. How the public sees the politician is of great concern to their political well-being, subsequent employment, and often may be the origin of many internal and external conflicts that require the political actor to wear many different masks to effectively communicate with society's varying audiences. This role-playing creates a means to an end relationship that requires many selves to exist within one body, a trait not unlike that of an employee trying to satisfy the boss—a trait that many political leaders have to possess in order to relate to and meet the demands of varying constituencies.

Those who occupy public positions are caught between their innate desire to lead and "order taking." Political laborers drive the political system whose task (supply) is to produce results based on society's demands. However, it was intended that the will of the people would be filtered through deliberative process, and that people of good will, serving as our representatives, would be able to use their experience and wisdom to temper public passion. Today, the deliberative process is conducted in a "fish bowl" the size of an aquarium. Public servants are public property, and rarely, from a privacy standpoint, can call anything theirs. A well-intended law, such as The Freedom of Information Act, makes public all phone calls and correspondence, while financial disclosure regulations make politicians' and their spouses' financial holdings and obligations public. Politicians' children are often photographed and their lives published. We increasingly see politicians' medical history or visits to the doctor on television. All of this scrutiny, much of which is necessary to ensure that ethics laws are adhered to, is intended to be a transparent part of our governmental process. However, much of today's scrutiny is for the pleasure of a tabloid-driven pastime. Due to this, it is increasing difficult for politicians to define themselves in an era where judgment is rendered in a millisecond, aided by the click of a computer mouse or view of a widescreen television. A politician's difficulty in defining themselves has dampened the ideological energy that emanates from not only an individual's core personality, but also that which is formed as a result of a vibrant deliberative process. This resulting ideological void has caused new conflicts, as political leaders desire to act on public opinion reflects expediency rather than deliberation, and this often clashes with their own personal set of doctrines and beliefs.

Historically, when a political leader expressed their own ideology, it would be a lightning rod for many of the conflicts within the political spectrum. Ben Franklin found that lightning—and its resulting energy—could be extremely useful. In the political arena, the energy that ignited this lightning bolt helps to form ideas, providing a nexus between those ideas, ideology, and action. Too often in our era, when political leaders express their view and ideas, they are quickly scorched by the ensuing reaction without deliberation by the media, as well as public and political foes. As a result of this third-degree experience, few leaders are willing to challenge the public with ideas that may be contrary to popular thinking. More often than not, the lack of "ideas" and subsequent political ideology leads to inertia.

Politicians develop an understanding of themselves mostly through their public activities. The conflict politicians often face is that who they are is often how they are seen. Introspection is sacrificed by public inspection. Tension exists between who a politician "is," who the public says they are, or who they demand them to be. Legislative "acts" require officials to process the fact that different strokes are required for different folks. Being all things to all people is a source of much cynicism and conflict leveled at politicians. The criticism stems from the electorate sensing insincerity from those who are not wedded to one particular constituency, along with fears that their views are often sacrificed in a process where their leaders maintain multiple selves. This is seen as a natural part of a social system where individuals serve as laborers/actors in order to execute specific actions that are the result of a means to end relationship.

There was a time when pubic service was viewed as a "calling." This principle was a fundamental part of our founding fathers' vision of public service. Our forefathers envisioned a political system where an ordinary citizen would temporarily leave their professional lives in order to answer a public service "calling," a principal fundamental to public service. By answering the "call," however, it was never intended that individual thought would be subservient to the demands of the public. Rather, that the needs of the public would be filtered through the experience and wisdom that the chosen public officials could provide through appropriate consultation. Today, however, an official often filters their thoughts through the anticipated reaction of the public. As a result, the nexus between collective consciousness and individual thinking is political identity and its resulting ideology. Political officials therefore engage in an internal process that takes into account the external collective voices of society in order to exercise actions that reflect their public identity. Individuals, however, are wrapped up in a myriad of different conflicts that stem from identity and an individual's difficulty in defining whom they are.

The conflicts that public officials face lie not only in the nature of their defined responsibilities, but also in how they are defined by themselves and their employer, the public. This duality of definition creates an internal and external struggle that adds to the fractious nature of our political system. While everyone feels the consequences of this, they are borne mostly by the politician who is a public servant and property, and as such, wrestles with the competing demands that are placed upon their shoulders—by themselves and the public.

COALITIONS

"One's intimate circle can change and the alignment of stars that can bring an adversary's coalition together can also produce a similar constellation in your orbit, at another time or place."

Michael J. O'Halloran

PEOPLE, like animals, tend to travel in packs. For those on the public stage, the journey is not traversed on foot, but rather in thought and action. It is in the formation of coalitions that officials, or members of the public, surround themselves with like-minded individuals, bringing to the arena either victory or defeat of another's proposals. The recognition of the kinship that exists within social and political cliques is an interdependent, identity-driven process. An individual's "public face" is expressed demonstrating the collaboration between oneself and their political group.

The role that individuals play in the public arena requires periodic adjustments made in order to fulfill the expectations of those within a given political group. These adjustments are often made with premeditation because of past experience. Knowing what positions other group members have taken in the past enables one to make the adjustments that will satisfy group members and allow an individual actor to advance to a leading role. This is often allowed by the tacit support of opponents, who clearly observed the transformation, but remain silent because today's enemies are often tomorrow's friends.

The coalition connection recognizes that one's intimate circle can change and the alignment of stars that can bring a adversary's coalition together can also produce a similar constellation in your orbit, at another time or place.

Two primary obligations exist inherently in community and elected actors. The first is to their relationships and the town itself, and the second is to your proposal. (More often than not, the two are linked, but it is up to you as the petitioner to demonstrate the linkage.) These obligations introduce the "public face" onto the public stage. This "public face" that officials wear is simply a role being played and lines being delivered, masking an individual official's true beliefs. Knowing this, members who recognize the performance taking place before them watch silently in order to prevent the disruption of underlying relationships. They choose not to "call-out" the masquerade for what it is, even when political or tactical expediency would dictate an unmasking.

In the political arena, individuals are defined by their actions. The mark created by what they do and to who is seemingly indelible. Public officials assert themselves on matters that concern other members or petitioners through "role playing." This method of "pleasing" constituencies forms the actor's "public self." The actions that a public official takes in relation to their outcomes have a direct effect on how the political actor is viewed. The labels that result from this—such as "liberal," "conservative," "tree-hugger," or "pro-development"—fix how the public and their colleagues see officials. The labeling that occurs can often stick for life and impair future relations. For instance, in Any Town, U.S.A., there is an older neighborhood consisting of homes that were built prior to current zoning laws. In this neighborhood, a property owner would like to tear down his home and build a new one with modern amenities and current safety requirements. The home is a single story 20' x 25' dwelling set on a piece of land that is 50' x 50'. The home is situated just five feet from its neighbor to the left. The homeowner would like to tear down the existing structure and position a new, two-story home in the center of the plot, creating 15 feet on either side. Local zoning laws in this neighborhood, however, require that any replacement home must be built on the footprint of the existing structure. The second story is permissible as long as the home is built in the same location. Current zoning laws ignore the neighbor's overwhelming support for the project. The public's interest in moving the home in order to create a balanced streetscape is disregarded. Once the matter is brought up before a board empowered to grant zoning relief in Any Town, a member of the board impresses upon his colleagues to deny the request by the petitioner to move his home. He argues, "If we do this, we will establish a precedent and have all sorts of people with requests coming before us. The situation can be correctly compared to a kindergarten teacher denying one student's request to go to the bathroom, based on her rationale "If I let one go, you will all want to go." The petitioner has now formed the impression that the public official is unreasonable and is not acting on behalf of his and his neighbor's interests. The officials' actions will determine how a petitioner will view the deliberative skills of that official. However, the petitioner who sits front row center at a performance will not be the only participant to form impressions from these experiences. Other participants, and those indirectly affected, will take the same impressions despite being up in the balcony. Actors on the public stage (elected, appointed, and petitioners) must recognize that they are seen and judged in the eye of the beholder.

The power of identity is as forceful as the

wheel that moves us forward. Its hub is the Self and its spokes are representative of all the varying facets of one's public and private life. Work, family, school, citizen, public official, spiritualist, and private thinker all come together to form who we are. The public identity of elected officials is often formed by the positions that those officials take. Taking no action or "fence-sitting," as it is commonly referred to, can also form public identity. This can be frustrating for the official whose intentions may be wrongly inferred by the public.

Neil Diamond sang, "'I am, I cried; I am said I." If only it were that simple. Unfortunately, we live in a world where if we are not able to define who we are, others are more than willing to do it for us. Opportunity exists, but not without consequences. How public officials are seen is dependent upon the subjective lens through which they are viewed by the electorate, media, and petitioners. In a political context, who we are depends on whom you ask.

In the film *Analyze This*, Billy Crystal's character is asked who he is and responds by saying: "Who am I? Who am I? Who am I? 'Who am I' is a question of the ages. That's one we're all searching for. The question is to find out who I am? To find out who I am 'who' wants to come out say I'm hungry… who I am is too deep. My name is Ben Sobel…lioni. Ben Sobellioni. I'm also known as, uh, Benny the Groin, Sammy the Schnazz, Elmer the Fudd, Tubby the Tuba, and once as Miss Phyllis Levine. But this has nothing to do with why I'm here with you fine gentlemen today. That being said, I'm also known by those who know the best as the @%*%!@ (rhymes with plucking) doctor," Like Crystal's character, we are often known in different ways by many people.

PUBLIC HEARING

"The public hearing process, as we commonly know it, is structured to be primarily a vehicle for "testimony," not dialogue. This structured process prevents the necessary interaction that is needed to ensure meaningful public involvement."

MICHAEL J. O'HALLORAN

DELIBERATIVE bodies are, by definition, charged with thoughtfulness in decision and action in assessing all sides of an issue. However, their assessment tools lack the calibration to properly measure and interpret public opinion. The tool of choice, while inadequate, is the public hearing process—inadequate because its intention (to hear) rarely reaches its destination (one's ears). One would think that public hearings would generate much "hearing" of the public's interest; that this is a process whereby people would be heard. But as Daniel Kemmis (1990) states, "In fact, out of everything that happens at a public hearing—the speaking, the emoting, the efforts to persuade the decision maker, the presentation of facts—the one element that is almost totally lacking is anything that might be characterized as public hearing."

This structure is the result that provides for public hearings. This structure, by design, places the expressing of interests secondary, if at all, to taking a position. From the outset, the public is asked to approach the podium as either a proponent or an opponent.

For example, in my community of Waltham, Massachusetts, *Waltham City Council Rule 29A* states: "The first 30 minutes, if needed, shall be set aside for proponents of the pending proposal to speak in favor of the proposal. If the testimony of all proponents takes less than 30 minutes, then the President shall, upon conclusion of their testimony, move on to hear testimony from opponents." This forces people to take sides and skews the hearing towards having "sides." Interests are lost in the process. Perhaps the makers of this rule thought it the best way to "frame" an understanding of the public's perspective.

However, perspective is formed based on the information that one has and their worldview. More often than not, those who take to the podium of public assertion use this forum to express who they are and how they see the world. This result is promoted by the reliance on standard procedures, such as rules that are meant to be applied in every situation, thereby limiting the scope of understanding that can be achieved. This not only frustrates petitioners, but the public as well. Citizens who simply wish to ask a question in a neutral manner are often prohibited from doing so from a neutral position. Public board rules often force people to take sides in order to gain access to the podium. Members of the public who may have varying interests are positioned into the adversarial roles of being either "proponents" or "opponents." It has been my observation that in these instances, people predominantly fall into the opponent camp, thereby skewing the weight of the sentiment in opposition. This inadvertent weighing often further separates parties into groups that have "their minds made up" and therefore no dialogue takes place.

The only measurement of public input is the counting of heads as being either for or against a proposal. Unfortunately, the public's only gauge to determine if they were "heard" will be the statements that a board member makes throughout the process and their ultimate vote on a petition—a decision that is reflective of the public's previously stated "position" as being a "proponent" or "opponent." Etched in stone, these numbers can alter the deliberative landscape.

This structured process prevents the necessary interaction that is needed to ensure meaningful public involvement, resulting in the formation of terrain that forces petitioners to travel in Public Litigation Vehicles (PLV). Forced off the road, petitioners are denied access to further formal channels of discussion with the public because the "hearing process" has concluded. Their only remedy is often the courts or some other appellate avenue, when a trip down Dialog Drive could avoid litigation, reduce conflict, and facilitate the expression of shared interests. The public hearing process, as we commonly know it, is structured to be primarily a vehicle for "testimony," not dialogue. This "devil's advocate" approach, where one party looks for an opportunity to exploit the weaknesses in another's argument, may be an appropriate means toward having opposing views cross at the intersection of information and argumentation, but collision is more likely. What we need is to have a colliding of interests that incorporates public need with the wants of the public. This want/need relationship is based on the "individual" wants of members of the public versus the needs of the public at large. For example, planners, demographers and economists can forecast and demonstrate the "need" for more housing, but individual community members may not want more housing because they are not in "want" of a place to live. It may be time that the town may need to update its zoning codes so that aging office parks can attract and meet the requirements that tenants require in today's marketplace. But members of the public who are not a prospective tenant may oppose the redevelopment effort simply because it does not meet their specific wants, even if it serves the larger community interest of an enhanced tax base and resulting benefits.

The challenge for our public officials is to balance the immediate wants of the public with the long term needs of the community.

> "While popular opinion was hardly irrelevant, it was regarded as flight, undependable, shortsighted, and easily manipulated. The ultimate allegiance of the founders was not to 'the people' but to 'the public,' which was the long-term interest of the citizenry…"
>
> *American Creation: Triumphs and Tragedies at the Founding of the Republic*: Joseph Ellis

Our public officials can not be expected to meet challenge of educating the public alone. Those who stand before the body politic seeking to advance a proposal must work with officials towards informing the public.

MEETING THE CHALLENGE

If the structure of our public boards limits discourse and encourages litigation, then those who are affected by its results need to lead, listen, and levitate in order to break the congestion that gridlocks the meeting of needs. As a petitioner, you can lead by setting the tone for your proposal. This begins by learning the underlying needs of all of the stakeholders. I'm not talking about identifying people's "positions"—such as "I'm for the environment, I'm against traffic (who isn't?), I'm against change"—but truly learning about all of the stakeholders (elected officials, community activists, neighborhood abutters, and bureaucrats [affectionately stated]) who may have to implement your proposal's underlying interests. Needs are both verbal and non-verbal. You must learn to key in on both stated and unmentioned needs.

Your approach is not that of a distributive negotiator: if you think they are in possession of a pie, then claim there is no pie; if the pie is in the middle of the table, they want it all; if forced to share the pie, they want to do the slicing as well as serving; if it must be split, then at least one party will be pie-deprived and it won't be them.

As a petitioner before a public board, you must be integrative not distributive. By leading with an integrative mind set, you understand that not only would you like to have some pie, but perhaps you and your guests (oh, did you forget, you won't be dining alone. There will be board members, community activists, municipal officials, and others at your table so you may want to roll out the dessert cart before any slicing begins.) Now I don't mean to suggest that by being an integrative facilitative leader your role is to serve up good treats and plenty of it, but it is not a good idea to begin by being good only to become bad and ugly.

You must throw away the script of coercion ("approve this or we'll see you in court"), the sales pitch script ("this is being done elsewhere"), and the good doctor script ("this medicine is good for you"). These catchphrases must be replaced by an integrative approach that seeks to inform rather than storm. By leading with integration, you can demonstrate the interdependent relationship between both you as the proponent of a project, idea or cause and the very people whose responsibility it is to give approval. Your actions from beginning to end must foster and safeguard this interdependent relationship.

This interdependent relationship that I speak of was once respected as the public and its officials recognized that private concerns could meet public needs. The proverbial "in my day" flashback reveals public/private partnerships that built highways, hospitals, and whole towns. This once idyllic collaboration that built America and shaped its policies is now used by proponents as a club to stop progress, even progress that seeks renewal through redevelopment, redevelopment not only of brick and mortar but proposals that seek to restructure public policy. The sentiment of our time must reflect the collaborative practices of the past. Today's communities must be built upon the foundations of the past, a foundation that allowed a nation to thrive when people worked together for a common purpose, meeting the needs of one another.

Your role as a petitioner, developer, infrastructure provider, or parent trying to advance curricula or improve the school lunch program, is to restore the partnership that once existed between public and private interest by educating community leaders on the benefits of collaboration. This collaborative process begins when you recognize that each side has needs lying beneath the surface of stated positions.

These needs must be explored by going beneath the surface stated demands of each party down to the unmentioned "real needs" of each party. By doing this, you're more likely to get others to tune in to your proposal. Yes, there will be the occasional sour note, but by being a facilitative leader you can do your part to craft an outcome that will be in harmony with everyone's needs.

Getting Your Proposal Heard Begins With Listening

Listening is something that you're doing right now, reading this and substituting the words on the page with a voice in your head. Is it my voice as the author of these words that you hear? Is it your own, a coworker's, a boss, or a first grade teacher? Each of us processes the words we hear or see through various filters. The filters can clean out clutter, making it easier to understand what is being said, but filters can also add bias as the communicative traffic flows through. Bias causes us to interpret a sender's message in a different way than intended. The unintentional receiving of information endangers our relationships and frames a portrait of one another that won't be hanging above the fireplace soon. If barriers to communication exist in everyday life, then how much more are they complicated by the procedural communication that exists when you, as a petitioner, appears before a public board? Human encounters can be wonderful; we give life to one another, support and share sorrow and joy. But encountering a clerk at the return desk at your favorite store, a neighbor who is encroaching on your land, or that old crank at the office can all be stressful. As a petitioner, you will be asking others to consider your proposal; for them and for you, this too can be stressful. The stresses that I define here lie in the concern that petitioners have as to how to best present their proposal to the public and the appointed decision makers. Any initial meeting between people, one who is asking for something and one who is granting something, are often met with a guarded reception. For the receiver of the information, the feeling is not unlike that of how you might feel when you walk into a car showroom and are greeted by a salesperson. You might brace yourself and think, "Here comes the sales pitch." You're skeptical, cautious, and yet confident that you will not be "sold" prematurely. At first, the salesperson is seen as your adversary. You think, "I'll wipe the floor with him" or "he won't take advantage of me." As a result, you listen as if each word is a guided missile, and you, like a soldier, attempts to counter the attack with your own verbal assault.

As a petitioner, you must be careful not to have encounters of the adversarial kind. Too often, both the petitioner and community decision makers find themselves seated at the proverbial chess table—each sizing up one another's next move and looking for a checkmate. I'm not saying that petitioners intend to play this game, but more often than not those on the community side of the table infer that your moves will advance a loss on their part. And as on the showroom floor at the car dealership, there exists stressors that taint what should be a meeting of interdependent needs (I'm selling, you're buying). An interdependent relationship exists between you, the petitioner, and those decision makers with whom you are interacting.

As a petitioner, you can be part of a "problem-solving process" instead of part of the "problem." You can transform existing political environments by first beginning to gather information and trying to understand the true interest of the concerned parties. Petitioners can enhance the existing systems and structures, and strive to improve the atmosphere of our decision-making bodies by creating conditions for learning. By encouraging concerned parties to express their interests and moving beyond taking positions, you can create an educative environment to not only improve the communication of the parities in the dispute, but also improve the general deliberative atmosphere.

The opportunity for enlightenment is greater when dialogue is taking place. A real estate developer may offer a compromise on the number of units they are seeking to build in order to gain approval. A proponent of a plan to lengthen the school day by two hours may reduce their proposal to one hour in order to find some middle ground. Both parties may often be dismayed that such offers of compromise give them no traction, because what is at stake for the community are deeply held values. Those offering the compromise see their offer as an act of good will and anticipate a positive reaction—or at the least the beginning of a negotiated settlement.

Petitioners who recognize the unique conflicts that exist for public officials can shape their proposal to reflect the deliberative culture and community character. Petitioners must also acquire the skills to demonstrate thoughtfulness in their actions. When confronted by those who express otherwise, do not treat them as fixed, but rather work with them to prevent them from viewing you as fixed. Transform unproductive thinking that leads to wasteful and hurtful actions into opportunities for the public arena to function well. Recognize and draw attention to positive actions, increasing their visibility. Participants can begin to transform their stated adversarial positions by giving voice to, and hearing, one another's underlying interests. By talking to each other rather than *at* each other, petitioners, public officials, and community members can learn the origins of their conflict. Those origins are both tangible and intangible. Absent open dialogue are unknown to each party and therefore irresolvable. Conflicts in the public arena have their origins in both the way public participation is structured and the identity-based issues that surround officials, the public, and you. As a petitioner, you must work within existing structures but you can begin with structuring your proposal and behavior that begins with the end in mind. How do you want to be thought of when the public process concludes? To what ends do you want to achieve? What will be the means for getting there? When our founders envisioned how our country would be governed, they created a landmark document that would not only serve as the law of the land but also shape our future. As a petitioner in the public arena, you will need to develop a personal constitution for being heard and understood in the public arena. Your personal constitution will provide a framework for "how" you, as a petitioner, trying to advance a proposal in the public arena will conduct yourself and advance your ideas. The constitution that you adopt must begin with a *preamble,* a declaration for action and attitude that lays out your personal affirmations for conducting yourself in the public arena.

In doing so, you will develop a better understanding of the body politic and assist those whom are guardians of the public good meet the needs of the public.

The following is an example of a personal constitution for getting heard and understood in the public arena.

PREAMBLE

As a petitioner before a public board, first seek to *understand* before trying to be understood. Focus on interests and not positions, neither posture nor provoke; provide facilitative leadership in order to give voice to stakeholders' concerns, hopes, and aspirations for their community. Listen actively and work to develop options around proposals while holding true to your aims. Provide alternatives and choices that foster community ownership of outcomes.

To ensure that proposals are purposeful and meet the public need, use an educative approach to *inform* rather than storm deliberative bodies. Solicit feedback and engage officials in meaningful dialog that begins with the end in mind, but is also mindful that the means to achieving "ends" must be participatory, process-driven, and integrative. Integrate what is said into actions that are dependable, verifiable, and nurture relationships. Recognize that any advancement of a proposal depends upon the interdependent nature that exists between you as the petitioner and the community that is deliberating on your proposal. Before the body politic, stand for ideas that seek to meet the public need. Acknowledge that "needs" can be viewed subjectively, and never take objection to differences in opinion that will inevitably arise. Rather, work toward reconciling difference by adding community viewpoints into proposals while subtracting out the temptation to be locked into original thought. Multiply thinking in order to meet the underlying concerns of all parties and yield outcomes that serve the public good.

FACILITATIVE LEADERSHIP

"When one hears of leadership, or more specifically, political leadership, one often looks for the ideology behind the leader. Facilitative leaders are driven by methodology, not ideology."

MICHAEL J. O'HALLORAN

A magician may pull a rabbit out of his hat, while we, the audience, see what has appeared, but do not know how it appeared. Unlike the magician, whose secrets are vital to his trade, the facilitative leader seeks to inform group members through example, and by sharing process skills, to enhance the deliberative environment. When one hears of leadership, or more specifically, political leadership, one often looks for the ideology behind the leader. Facilitative leaders are driven by methodology, not ideology. Their passion is not in what gets done, but in how it is done. The "how" improves the quality and effectiveness of the "what," and in doing so, it reduces conflicts by enabling varying ideological forces to converge without colliding.

Similar to navigators who help disoriented travelers arrive at their desired destination, facilitative leaders impart influence through their actions and behaviors, making it possible for fractious factions to reach a resolution. To achieve this objective, facilitative leaders influence existing process, established by the body politic that you stand before. In the 1957 film *12 Angry Men*, we find a jury impatiently ready to declare a young boy guilty of murdering his father and sentence him to death. The jury initially voted 11-1 in favor of the boy's guilt, but become frustrated that one member vote of "not guilty" would hold up the process of declaring the boy guilty. The 11 jurors then challenge the lone juror, played by Henry Fonda, for casting a vote of "not guilty." They chastised Fonda, "How can you say he is not guilty?" "With all the evidence, why would you let a murderer go free?" Fonda's character responded by saying that he did not know whether he was guilty or innocent, just that he felt that if a person's life would be at stake, as a result of a jury vote, then the least we ought to do is "talk about it."

Fonda's character was not the foreman of the jury. He did not occupy any formal role of authority. He was in the minority opinion and standing alone against an angry mob. Not wanting to follow, he chose to lead. He did this not from the authoritative position of jury foreman, but as a facilitative leader.

He engaged the jurors with examples of how it could be possible that the boy was not guilty and established a process for deliberation. This lone juror in an early dramatic scene produced a knife out of his pocket in order to demonstrate that it was a similar knife to the one the boy was accused of uniquely possessing and had used such a unique knife to kill his father. Fonda's character's drama served to catch the attention of the angry jurors long enough for him to persuade them that they must follow a process. That evidence must be sifted through carefully and methodically, not judged based on ideology or bias.

Fonda's character's fidelity was to the process, not the outcome. He assumed a leadership position by facilitating a process for deliberation. He served as the leader of the group even though he did not occupy a position of formal authority. His role was to facilitate *how* the jury would reach a decision not *what* decision they would reach.

As a facilitative leader, you will….

Section One:
Model

You can make contagious the importance of "good process" by walking the talk. Establish the tone, direction, and dialog that your proposal will be conveyed with by making your behavior an example to be followed. By your active engagement in productive behavior, you can bring parties together. This will establish your intent to foster a collaborative atmosphere from the beginning. Understand the specific issues that are important to each party.

Section Two:
Focus

Maintaining focus on the process can be challenging as divergent issues arise. Pay attention to how your meeting will be structured—issue management, time held, speaking sequencing, location, expert or third part testimony, and hearing and receiving opposing views. Be ever mindful of the fact that what you want to achieve depends on how you do it.

Section Three:
Atmospherics

Where you meet and with whom will set the tone for discourse, and ultimately for the course that lies ahead. Make sure to meet with all interested parties and work together to agree upon meeting places and times, and to ensure that the meeting space is arranged appropriately so that an "us vs. them" arrangement is avoided. Manage differences by providing an opportunity to redefine by example how people view things. Seat parties so that dialog is encouraged.

Section Four:
Create

Initiating a communicative process that aims toward

fixing problems, rather than affixing blame, will ultimately create an environment that is conducive to effective decision-making. Through this "process," all of the participants are better equipped to focus on the "content" of your proposal rather than the political dynamics. The communication process is not an accessory. Wear its importance on your shirtsleeve—fashion all agreements around an effective communication continuum.

Section Five:
Understand

Effective leaders know their flock, often rise up through the ranks. Working as a petitioner who practices leadership, your role is informal. Know the core values of the community and the groups that you are working with.

Section Six:
Empower

By recognizing the point of view of all parties, you allow others to move beyond a singular subjective viewpoint and toward a new, shared paradigm. Your proposal not only should be purged of any divergent views, but also should remain open and flexible, and not under an unwavering, fixed mindset.

Section Seven:
Facilitate

Pay careful attention to the mix of procedures and relationships that make up facilitation. By understanding and recognizing the roles that individuals play, you can establish an aura of respect amongst all parties. Understand that individual roles are often interdependent and that your proposal is dependent on them.

Section Eight:
Lead

Leadership is commensurate with influence. This influence, however, begins first by understanding those that you seek to lead. By listening actively and observing the environment and its members, you can recall behaviors and conversations while simultaneously identifying similarities and differences, recognizing different perspectives, and giving accepting feedback. The information relative to your proposal should be shared in a manner that will permit others to understand it. When others follow your lead, decisions can be reached through a deliberative process, rooted in inclusion rather than the authoritarian approaches of their ideological counterparts. Seek first to understand in order to be understood.

COMMUNICATION

☞ **Article One** — Communication is more than the simple act of transmission. The exchange of ideas and messages in order to advance one's interests is often a perilous endeavor. People who are shaped by experience, culture, and genetics add meaning and interpretation to any information provided. For the receiver of information, the addition of personal bias, fears, and aspirations distort the message being sent. Inferences are drawn that the sender never intended to have inferred. In the public arena, there are multiple personalities that increase the distortion of the message that is being sent. The challenge for the speaker is to ensure that their message is being received as intended.

Section One:
Consult

As a petitioner in the public arena, you must first consult those who will be in the arena with you. Consider all public officials, citizen groups, neighbors, business people, and anyone directly impacted by your proposal.

Section Two:
Relate

By connecting your proposal to community needs, you further the interdependent nature that exists between you, your proposal, officials, and the community members that they represent. Share information as to why your proposal serves the community.

Section Three:
Indicate

Civility and working together are part and parcel of collaboration and are not necessarily indicative of agreement. Recognize that good relations are not a sign of agreement or acceptance.

Section Four:
Dictate

Telling officials what to do can be interpreted by those in authority as a declaration of their public failures. Never dictate or impose authority on anyone, especially those in authority.

Section Five:
Articulate

It is through productive and open communication that parties can begin to understand and resolve differences. Be aware that people see things differently, because after all, "How can we solve problems if we do not know how another sees things."

Section Six:
Rapport

Your proposal will inevitably go through a ratification process, resulting in a document that is reflective of community interests and concerns. Build rapport through emotional affinity and by structuring proposals that affirm your relationship.

Section Seven:
Reliability

Your incorporation of actions that seek to remedy individual and collective issues in your proposal will be the cornerstone on which your reliability will be judged. Implement agreements and solicit feedback. Verify, prior to implementation, that actions are meeting intentions. Be consistent in thought and in actions.

Section Eight:
Feedback

The shared experiences gained by the give and take of feedback facilitates problem solving and genuine understanding. Ask questions that get to the underlying interests. Go beneath a person's stated positions to discover what they are "really saying."

ROAD BLOCKS

☞ **Article Two** — Doctors take an oath that requires them to "do no harm." Intervene, but make sure that a procedure makes better, not worse. When communicating, we all run the risk of putting up unintended barriers or creating roadblocks that impede our ability to get through to another person. Public communication is particularly treacherous. While the road ahead is paved with good intentions, it is riddled with steep inclines and "S" curves. Travelers are aware that the officials, the public, and the media are watching them. Traveling in a thickly settled district, you must adjust your speed to conform to the neighborhood conditions and to proceed with caution. Keep your eye on the road because at any moment someone or something may jump out in front of you, or more than likely your actions will unintentionally collide with the merging of vehicular ideas and interests. The responsibility to avoid a collision is yours.

In the public arena, defensiveness can run high. There exists a great deal of community pride, individual authorship of legislation, and a weight of expectation that rests upon the shoulders of officials trying to balance constituent expectations with practicality. Community values and its collective self-esteem are present and protected by political infrastructure. As a petitioner, never diminish the importance of communication and be ever vigilant not to do the following:

Section One:
Threaten

It is often counterproductive to juxtapose your proposal with alternatives that threaten. Making statements such as, "if you don't do this…we will go to court, or build waste treatment facility on the site, or run people against you in the next election," often turns a problem to be solved into a battle to be won. Never threaten those who you stand before.

Section Two:
Evaluate

Evaluation is a tricky tool. Used appropriately, evaluation can be constructive and appreciated: "Looking over your local by-laws, I noticed that the original framers stated that no building shall have anything hang over the roofline. I would suggest to the current board that this be amended to allow for gutters so that the water can drain off to the side in a controlled manner, so that no one passing beneath will get injured when icicles form in the winter." However, evaluation can also be taken as an insult and place officials in the position of finding it necessary to save face: "You people ought to…" Recognize that passing judgment is a ruling that is rarely in order.

Section Three:
Stereotype

Making global generalizations such as, "You people are all on the take," or "Bureaucrats! You don't know what it's like in the real world," can often be detrimental to your cause. Although the statements may be true in some cases, they are not necessarily transferable from community to community. Do not assume that what was acceptable to one governing body is necessarily acceptable to another.

Section Four:
Publicly Diagnose

Analyzing publicly why an official or citizen is taking the position or action that they are taking is yet another downfall. By making public statements like, "You're only doing this because…" you run the risk of misdiagnosing someone's intentions. Don't inject your analysis of official's behavior onto the public stage.

Section Five:
Condition

Never make doing good deeds a condition of an agreement: "If you approve the building of the supermarket, we promise to keep the parking lot clean." Making good behavior a condition of an agreement takes the good out of the behavior.

Section Six:
Discourage

All thoughts are relevant because they impact decision-making. People should never be dissuaded from expressing their point of view. Unmentioned thoughts—those that are not vocalized—are even more important in many cases. People often keep these thoughts front and center in their minds, acting on them without reaping the benefits that open communication can bring through clarification. Many people prefer to discuss privately before going public with a thought or suggestion. Make yourself available to receive and share information with another person, and allow for personal exchange rather than public.

Section Seven:
Use Only Logical Argument

By using logic, you assume that others will share you view of the facts. Logical argument, however, is just one part of the equation. Logical argument should not be used alone to advance an idea without taking into consideration emotion, the other half of the equation. For example, you may have a proposal that will yield a town a much-needed tax revenue. However, what you're proposing may be viewed as more costly in terms of community identity and quality of life. Recognize that an individual's bias pervades all thinking and renders logic subservient to emotion.

Section Eight:
Put Ends Before Means

How you get to an agreement is as important as what you agree upon. The quality, effectiveness, and durability of decisions are greatly impacted by how decisions are made. Always put process ahead of product.

Be Reliable

Your consistency both in word and deed is essential to forging relationships and agreements. An official's comfort level with you and your ideas is dependent upon your honesty, clarity, and follow through. Carry out both in spirit and in practice what is agreed upon—never be unreliable.

LISTEN

☞ **Article Three** — In the late 1980's, the band Mike + the Mechanics wrote a song called "The Living Years." One of the key refrains said, "Can you listen as well as you hear?" People often state "I heard what you said," but are they truly listening to the thoughts, concerns, and emotion that are being conveyed?

Listening in the public arena will involve more than hearing. People tend to listen through their fears, not their ears. You need to convey to the speaker that you understand the significance of what they are stating.

Section One:
Listening

The listening process requires engagement. Your active participation furthers understanding and ultimately problem solving. Therefore, you must listen actively, not reactively. In a non-defensive manner, listen to what a speaker is saying from their perspective, not from yours. Do not get frustrated when you do not hear what you want. Have a desire to understand and interpret what is being said from the speaker's perspective. Encourage the speaker to continue by saying, "Tell me more about that."

Section Two:
Reflecting

In your own words, demonstrate to those you are communicating with that you heard both the words and sentiments that they are conveying: "I see that you are frustrated with the plan that I have put forth." Be a reflection in the mirror of the feeling and emotions that are in front of you.

Section Three:
Paraphrasing

By giving a concise account of what another speaker says, you can provide an opportunity for the speaker to clarify your interpretation of their words: "So what I hear you saying is that you are concerned how this proposal might impact the environment." The speaker may reply, "It's not just the environment per se, such as air quality, etc, but how your proposal may impact the character of the neighborhood." Never hesitate to repeat back in short form what others had to say, it will help you in the end.

Section Four:
Demonstrating Comprehension

Show officials and members of the public that you understand their views by putting their thoughts into action: "What I hear you saying is that you are concerned with traffic in your neighborhood. Why don't we commit to a study that will look at existing conditions and what impact this proposal will have in the future?" By giving other people's ideas a chance to work, you demonstrate not only that you heard them, but also that you are willing to "test out" and evaluate their suggestion. Walk the talk even if the journey is a road ultimately not to be taken.

Section Five:
Measuring Intensity

When passions are running high, it is important to take a moment to assess how best to proceed. First, you must acknowledge the significance of what is being conveyed. Some issues may affect community members directly and personally. If the city takes their home to make room for a new medical center, they will have to move, and their sentimental connection to the property will be dissolved. It may be appropriate to say in this case,

"Why don't we take a break so that we can talk about this directly?" Never plow though process at the expense of emotion. Attend to emotion, for emotion governs action.

Section Six:
Seeking Experts

When you are required to give an answer beyond your expertise, it is advantageous to bring in people who have knowledge expertise in that given area. By doing this, you allow the speaker to recognize that you take their concerns seriously: "I hear that you are concerned with potential air pollution that might be caused by tearing down the old chemical factory. We can hire air quality experts who will monitor the air during the demolition process and take steps to mitigate any problems." Recognize that what you don't know is often more important than what you do. Hire people who know.

Section Seven:
Recognizing

Often, your body language can exhibit your listening skills. Your posture, facial expressions, eye contact, and even your breathing, can speak much louder than the words that are coming from your mouth. Whether you are at a podium, a conference table, or a coffee shop, maintain a posture that suggests you are approachable, open to ideas, and interested in both sides of the story. Responding with physical empathy, such as a light touch on another's forearm, or a placement of your hand on a shoulder, creates connections that words alone cannot. Acquaint yourself physically so that your gestures support your words.

ASSERTION

☞ **Article Four** — When our nation's founders authored the preamble to the Constitution, they utilized this method of communication to declare their vision and purpose in a personal and rational manner. This declaration made by our forefathers granted neither to them, nor to a new nation, any powers, but served to explain its purpose. Assertion is not domination, but rather a reflection of liberation in action. As a petitioner before the body politic, the assertion of your proposal does not assume an end result is granted, but proposes how needs can be met and satisfied in accordance with consultation and legislation.

When expressing your plan….

Section One:
Articulate Purpose

It is fundamental that you convey your direction, the needs you are trying to meet, and the intended effects of your proposal. Express your ideas with clarity by letting those that you stand before know your motivation for being there.

Section Two:
Formulate

In the deliverance of your message, you should never shoot an accusation at another person or legislation in order to justify your proposal. Do not cast blame on another for existing circumstances, but rather formulate your message as a solution to unmet needs.

Section Three:
Deliver

How your proposal reaches the ears of decision makers and interested parties go a long way towards how it will be received. Did they hear about your proposal first or second hand? If second hand, did they feel left out? Was your message conveyed accurately? Was the phrasing and intended effect of your proposal correctly relayed? State your message in terms of meeting community needs and affirming community values, while remaining dedicated to delivering it in a manner that will ensure it is received as intended.

Section Four:
Have No Ifs, Ands, or Buts

First and foremost, a message should be stated in positive terms that demonstrate how it is fulfilling a community need. This being the case, you should never react to initial criticism by making your behavior contingent upon their reaction. Make your behavior unconditionally productive and assertive.

Section Five:
Avoid Lecturing

Officials and community members play a unique role in your proposal. Recognize them as individuals and the official positions that they occupy. When asserting your point of view, do so from your own perspective: "Speaking for myself I feel that…" Such statements minimize making assumptions regarding how others feel by reducing defensiveness and provoking the possible response of: "You don't speak for me" or "That is not how we feel." As I stated before, talk to people not at them.

Section Six:
Do Not Accuse

Always speak about needs and what you can do to meet them. Be careful not to "tell" official and community members what you want to do. Telling can be heard as a command, or as an accusation of what the community has not done correctly. Affirm the opportunity that you are presenting.

Section Seven:
Share

By dividing responsibility, you can create positive change. The vision for your proposal will need to be viewed with farsightedness. Looking into the future at a proposal's impacts is a joint endeavor. Share with others how you came up with your proposal, and how you processed existing circumstances to your present stance. Move others towards recognizing the interdependent relationship that exists between the parties.

Section Eight:
Restate

You will undoubtedly be receiving a great deal of feedback on your proposal. After you receive this feedback, incorporate suggestions that are consistent with your goals. Restate your proposal in evolved terms.

Section Nine:
Relevance

Stay on track to keep your message from being diverted by those who will use your proposal as a vehicle for their agenda. When confronted by diversion, acknowledge the remarks of the speaker, look for relevance, review the facts, and consider the emotion behind the statements. If you do not find a connection between the remarks and your proposal, ask, "How could my proposal reflect your concerns?" Look for the relevance between community concerns and your proposal.

Section Ten:
Resonate

Your proposal at this stage should capture the emotion, beliefs, and underlying interests of the community. Correspond closely with official and community members in order to produce a shared result.

PROBLEM SOLVING

Resolving differences between petitioners and the communities that they stand before requires an integrative process. Problems should be viewed as an opportunity to work together, not as a battle to be won. Solutions require trial and error, engagement, and evaluation. Harnessing the power from their collective insight, parties can begin ordered, deliberate, and honest communication. By acting jointly, parties can begin to understand the reasoning beneath one's stated positions. The unearthing of underlying interests alone presents a significant opportunity to advance problem solving. What may have seemed at the outset to be irresolvable can be transformed as parties learn of both the intangible and tangible factors in each other's initial positions. Divergent issue can be merged into tangible and verifiable agreements.

You can work collaboratively by…

Section One:
Disentangling

Disentangling the web of tension that is often created by the intermingling of political, social, and substantive issues requires an awareness of the individual threads that make up community fabric. Each issue needs to be dealt with separately before they are brought together and woven into an agreement.

☞ Clause One —

Separate the structure of the deliberative body from how it conducts its affairs.

☞ Clause Two —

Identify the correlation between getting things done in a political setting and the political characteristics exhibited by its members.

☞ Clause Three —

Partisan perceptions are derived from individual and or represented views.

☞ Clause Four —

Substantive concerns such as economic impact, traffic, and building codes are often the easiest to address, but remain a hurdle because the raising of such issues masks underlying political and social considerations. Be as committed to solving these concerns, as you are their more tangible counterparts.

Section Two:
Building Relationships

Relationships are often born from shared experience, but sometimes are also made contingent upon outcomes, holding them hostage to measurable gains. Make your relationships independent from substantive goals.

☞ Clause One —

Relationships are critical to human functioning. Treat them with respect and as a process in and of themselves.

☞ Clause Two —

Substantive issues should be addressed through persuasion not coercion.

☞ Clause Three —

Agreements reached through coercive means are not as durable because there is increased likelihood that the coerced party will seek to annul or place restriction on your proposal.

☞ Clause Four —

Know the difference between agreement and implementation. The coerced party, through other measures that require their approval in the future, will remedy what is agreed to coercively.

☞ Clause Five —

Coercion endangers relationships by reducing trust and interdependency.

☞ Clause Six —

Short-term goals should never be reached at the expense of long-term interest.

Section Three:
Understanding Partisan Perceptions

Partisan perceptions are present in all human interactions, and ignoring them can be perilous. You can reduce the risk of making assumptions by looking at the process used by others when they formed their perceptions.

☞ Clause One —

Induce attitude changes through persuasion by appealing to reason and addressing emotion.

☞ Clause Two —

Understand that emotions are idiosyncratic. Emotion follows thinking and perception. A person's views are subjective, and follow past experiences, confirm fears, and are filtered so they are congruent with their point of view: "This proposal reminds me of…"

☞ Clause Three —

Transforming how people "see things," as well as their subsequent emotions begins first with your "seeing things" from their point of view. Do not judge the rightness or accuracy of their views, but rather understand their origins. Partisan perceptions are subject to persuasion when you understand how they were formed.

☞ Clause Four —

Appeal to reason by not making your request contingent upon the other party abandoning their underlying convictions. Demonstrate the rationale for your proposal, how you developed it, and the logic for its existence.

Section Four:
Contemplation

☞ Clause One —

Provide the other party with information that will make your proposal appropriate for the community. Examine how the proposal addresses underlying needs, and highlight its advantages over other alternatives and existing or historical uses.

☞ Clause Two —

Share your thinking with the other party. Clarify how you came up with your proposal, why it was ruled in, and what was ruled out. Do not ignore how it addresses public needs, or its advantages over other options and existing conditions.

☞ Clause Three —

Recognize that the community fabric, and the stitch that you want to add, is woven together by at least three separate, but intertwined threads: your proposal, community issues, and the shared circumstance that is created when both you and the body politic intersect.

☛ **Clause Four —**

Work to align interests by detailing how your proposal meets the needs of the public based on your research, and invite them to share their parochial views and experience. Ask, "Is there anything that you could add based on your experience and knowledge of the area and people?" or "Can this proposal further enhance the needs of the community in any way?" By asking questions, you demonstrate to officials that while your proposal needs to meet certain economic, social, or practical benchmarks, how you will get there is flexible, and can be enhanced by their expertise.

Section Five:
Dealing With Differences

The Public Arena is particularly challenging because officials are composed of people from all backgrounds, coming from their "day job" to the public arena to do "the people's business." Officials have such diverse experiences, that it would not be unusual for a computer technician, a baker, and a candlestick maker to comprise a public board. These same diverse officials must then represent the public, which is even more diverse and typically only engaged in public policy on a transactional basis when issues directly affect them. This diversity furthers differences and challenges the problem resolution process.

☞ Clause One —

Begin to solve problems by first defining them in a manner that each party agrees upon. It may be wise to agree to have a third party craft a problem definition statement in order to minimize partisan perceptions. For example, if your proposal is for a development, and the community disagrees with your expert's judgment that it will be environmentally safe, than both parties may agree to have an independent review by outside experts. Whether it is an independent party, or the parties themselves, problems should be identified in a clear and concise manner that is easily understood by the public. Such a statement should also identify what mitigation or actions can be taken to address and resolve stated problems.

TIME TO GOVERN

FOR those who reside outside of the political system's elective or appointive positions, the opportunity to govern is limited. More often than not those on the outside are affected by a governing body's actions but rarely are able to shape the actions that are taken.

As a petitioner—or better still, a now informed petitioner—you can unfurl the knowledge that you have obtained to better govern your behavior and to improve the deliberative process.

I.
Seek to Understand

In life and particularly in the public arena, we expend lots of time and energy trying to be understood but not enough time trying to understand others. Make sure that you understand the interests of all parties involved and remember that interests often lie beneath one's stated positions. Someone may state that they are against your proposal to construct an addition to your home. Their stated position is one of opposition, but why? However, their underlying interest is a concern that your construction crew will be parking in front of their home and causing a disruption, which may extend to the time when they will be hosting guests in their back yard for their daughter's upcoming wedding party. Identifying their underlying concerns will allow you to work with your neighbor to mitigate any problems and gain their support. Identifying underlying interest is not easy, you must build trust, demonstrate a willingness to understand and share your interests openly. Doing so can make the difference between shouting at the wind and being heard.

II.
Identify the Unique Characteristics of the Deliberative Environment

Like a snowflake or a fingerprint each deliberative body has unique properties, even when its structure appears similar to other governing boards. A board that you are appearing before may have a similar charter for governance, i.e., the number of people on a board, term of office, etc. But how those who govern carry out their business is distinct. As a petitioner you need to grow to understand and appreciate the manner in which a particular body conducts its business by examining precedents, observing how members interact with one another and whether or not you are appearing before a body that is problem causing or problem solving.

III.
Utilize the BATABS
(Best Alternative To A By-Right Situation)

Every proposal should be measured against what is presently existing or allowable under law (By Right). You may be looking at redeveloping a site where an automotive repair shop is currently located. Your intention is to build a family restaurant. What is allowed "by right" as listed in the Zoning Manual of the town includes such things as fast food restaurants, night clubs and other uses that generate more traffic, litter and noise than your proposal for a family dine-in restaurant. Therefore, your proposal should be framed in such a way that encourages officials to consider it in light of alternatives. Go into the public arena with a clear sense of how your proposal measures up against what is allowed by right.

IV.
Address Contradiction by Adding Value

There is an old saying that making laws is like making sausage: you wouldn't want to see how it's done. To the untrained observer, the political arena is often home to many contradictions. For those who watch public boards conduct their business, contradiction may appear to be ever present. When you learn of the underlying reasons of why actions are taken in one case, but not in another, you can begin to appreciate and learn from the contradiction. By understanding another's underlying interest you can improve discourse and deliberation. Unfortunately, many petitioners who stand before the body politic seek to claim value ("My proposal will bring in millions of dollars a year in new tax revenue") as a means to overcome objections that may appear be contradictory to past actions officials may have taken. Rather, petitioners should create value ("My proposal will bring in millions of dollars a year in new tax revenue. By working with the town, this proposal, when completed, will add to the tax base, improve a blighted area, provide much needed housing, and bring more consumers into our downtown").

V.
Manage the Intangibles

As in most cases of disagreement, intangible factors are likely to be the puppeteer pulling the strings of the marionette on the public stage. It will take poignant questioning in order to unmask the truth behind stated positions that are often stated in tangible terms but the motivation behind them are often intangible. For example, you may be petitioning a public board to adopt a proposal to deem a certain section of town an "Economic Development Zone." During the process you come across a public official who is vehemently opposed to the creation of such a zone. The official's publicly stated position is that the proposal for an Economic Development Zone would lead to massive overdevelopment and congestion. What underlies this substantive position is the intangible factor of control. You see, as written, the proposed new zone would lessen the control that the current board has regarding development in that area. Having knowledge of such intangibles will help you to more specifically address people's real concerns.

VI.
Manage Factions

We began this book by looking at James Madison's thoughts on the influence of factions or alliances in society. He cautioned that even "enlightened statesmen" were subject to the pressure that factions can exert on the body politic. As a petitioner you need to work with the various coalitions that are not only within the public arena but surround it.

VII.
Keep Your Word

We live in an age where commitments must be backed up with action in order to build trust and reputations. Roy Lewicki tells us that "Reputations are like eggs- fragile, important to build, easy to break, and hard to rebuild once broken." In the public arena it is important that intention is followed up with action. Govern your behavior by the promises that you make. Be reliable, principled and keep your word.

VIII.
Evaluate and Address Differences

Be aware that the political arena requires compromise. After all politics is the art of compromise. However, one must be rational and practical when settling differences. Keep in mind that what may appear to be reasonable may not be seen as fair to all parties. Defining the "right thing" is often debatable. Look upon debate as a positive process not a battle to win. Often we care more about getting an idea passed than doing the right thing. Maintain an evaluative mindset in order to ensure that what is ultimately approved is what you sought in the first place.

AS I said in the opening, we have two ears and one tongue, therefore we should listen twice as much as we speak. We use our ears and mouth as tools for verbal communication. I hope that this book serves as a resource for more substantial communication in the public arena. Developing and honing your interpersonal skills will enable you to not only communicate more effectively with people, but perhaps even inspire them. Your confidence, knowledge, and ability to deliver a message clearly and succinctly—whether speaking before congress, a public board at city hall, or before the board of directors of your condominium or neighborhood association, will lead you to advance proposals and get heard.

ABOUT THE AUTHOR

Since his election as his hometown's youngest-ever City Councilor, **Michael J. O'Halloran** has compiled an encyclopedic knowledge of the inner workings of national, state and local government. He is, quite simply, a master of community-based issues, including the fine art of building trust and understanding between citizens and their government.

Michael's experience spans business, education and government. As evident in this book, he's been on both sides of the table—offering tough questions as an elected official and providing education, guidance and action to all. He employs numerous techniques including facilitation, negotiation, mediation and training. His hands-on approach aims to reduce conflicts, improve discourse and attain desired goals.

Michael O'Halloran holds a Master's Degree in Conflict Resolution from the McGregor School at Antioch University, and a Bachelor of Science from Suffolk University in Industrial/Organizational Psychology. He is a certified mediator and faculty member at Bentley University. His undergraduate students learn the art of Negotiation, Leadership, Organizational Behavior and Interpersonal Relations. Additionally, Michael has served as a Conflict Resolution Trainer at Brandeis University.

His public career includes over 25 years in elected

and appointed office, including service as member of the Waltham City Councilor—four years as City Council President and two terms on the Waltham School Committee. He served as Director of Public Affairs with a regional Chamber of Commerce and as a Legislative Aide to the Massachusetts House of Representatives. In addition, Michael has held senior policy-making positions with the Massachusetts Office of the State Auditor and the Massachusetts State Treasurer's Office.

In the private sector, Michael is the Principal Practitioner of Consensus Services specializing in community conflict management and he is frequently retained by political candidates and nationally recognized development, retail and service corporations.

Michael O'Halloran is an engaging and convincing public speaker. Using innovative narrative techniques, he has given countless presentations and talks in public forums covering subjects as varied as those discussed in *Lend Me Your Ear.* To inquire about his availability to speak in your area, please contact his office at:

michael@consensusservices.com